PUPPY BOWL

PUPPY BOWL

BOWL

THE BOOK

 Three Rivers Press • New York

Published in the United States by Three Rivers Press, an imprint of the Crown Publishing Group, a division of Penguin Random House LLC, New York.

www.crownpublishing.com

Three Rivers Press and the Tugboat design are registered trademarks of Penguin Random House LLC.

Animal Planet, Puppy Bowl, and logos are trademarks of Discovery Communications, LLC, used under license.

Library of Congress Cataloging-in-Publication Data is available upon request.

ISBN 978-0-553-41959-7
eBook ISBN 978-0-553-41960-3

Printed in China

Photographs by Discovery Communications
Cover design by Tal Goretsky
Cover photographs: (beagle, bottom left dog) Linn Currie/Shutterstock; (top right dog) Aaron Aldrich Fine Art/Getty Images; (top left dog) retales botijero/Getty Images; (stadium) Aksonov/Getty Images; (stadium lights) Evgeny Kuklev/Getty Images; (bottom right dog) Discovery Communications

10 9 8 7 6 5 4 3 2 1

First Edition

This book is dedicated to all the
wonderful animals in the shelter system
still looking for their forever homes,
and to the remarkable people who dedicate
their lives to caring for them

INTRODUCTION

Whether you're a football diehard or couldn't care less, when winter comes around, there's one game nobody wants to miss.

No, not the Super Bowl. The Puppy Bowl, of course!

On February 6, 2005, Animal Planet launched the cutest show on turf—*the* Puppy Bowl. And before long, what started as the ultimate showcase of the most adorable athletes on four legs soon grew into a true phenomenon. As it turns out, everyone loves puppies. "It seems to have found its audience," said Melinda Toporoff, executive producer of the *Puppy Bowl.*

It sure has. And now wagging tails, wet noses, fuzzy scrums, and packs of happy and hopping puppies

have become as much a Super Bowl Sunday tradition as seven-layer dip and pizza delivery. In fact, for many the Puppy Bowl has become the main attraction. After all, where else can you find dozens of little dogs that "compete" in the cutest of ways, frolicking and fumbling around a mini football field. Unlike the Super Bowl, everyone wins at the Puppy Bowl, no matter the score— even cat people. Did we mention there are kittens at halftime?

Since that first Puppy Bowl in 2005, the annual event has only gotten bigger and better. Now for the first time, the cutest puppies and most memorable scenes from Puppy Bowls over the years have been collected in one book.

So sit back and enjoy these classic Puppy Bowl moments!

FIRST HALF

The Bark Brothers form a ferocious backfield.

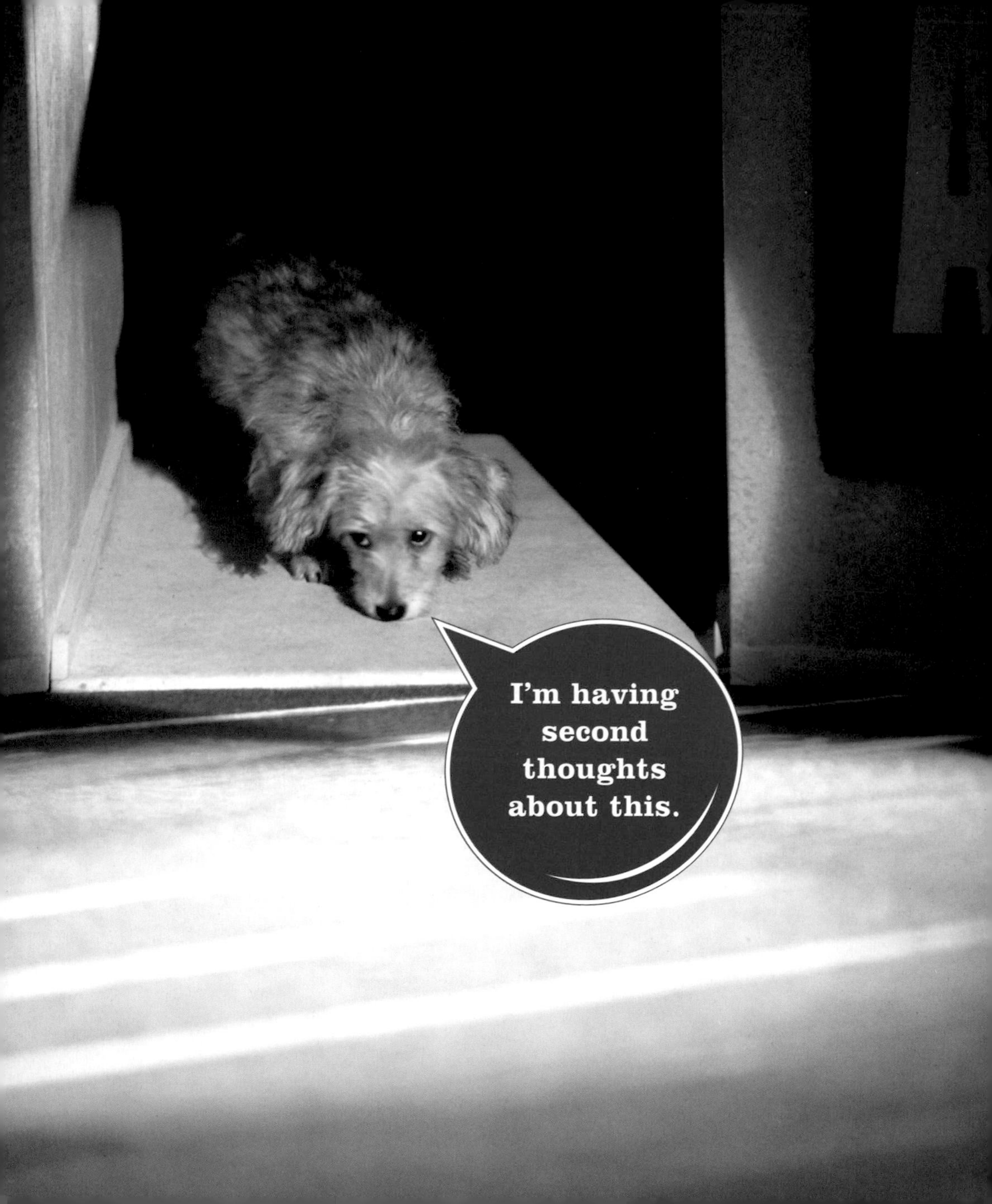
I'm having second thoughts about this.

TIME-OUT

WHY SO SERIOUS?

Ol' Blue Eyes

Face painter

FIRST HALF

BACK TO THE ACTION

Turning on the speed

30

TIME-OUT

STILL SO SERIOUS?

20

Downward Dog

FIRST HALF

BACK TO THE ACTION

Struttin' his stuff

Triple trouble

Sideline meeting

The last line of defense

Getting a time-out

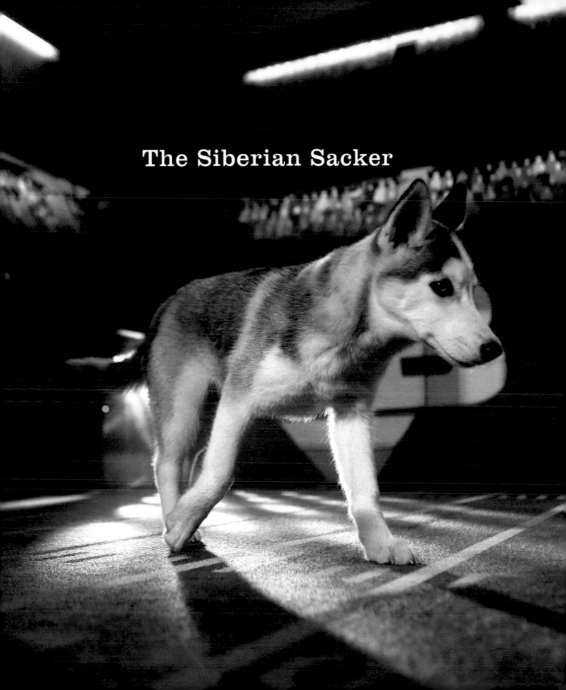

The Siberian Sacker

TIME-OUT

LITTLE FURBALLS

Poof!

Very huggable

Power puff

FIRST HALF

BACK TO THE ACTION

On the march

Built like a linebacker

HALFTIME

WHO NEEDS BANDS?

Halftime extravaganza

Pigskin cheerleaders

Half-time show stage fright

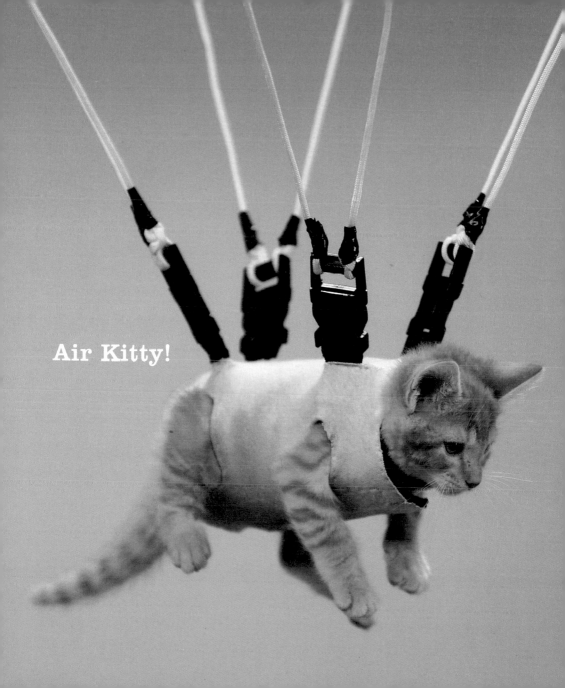

Air Kitty!

HALFTIME

Penguins on ice

Bright lights, little kitty

SECOND
HALF

Cuts to the outside

Breaks free up the middle

30

TIME-OUT

STRUTTIN' THEIR SCRUFF

20

Is that collar regulation?

SECOND HALF
BACK TO THE ACTION

They're one-on-one in the open field.

No place to go

Racing down the sideline

The defense bites on the fake, and he's in the clear.

He could . . . go . . . all . . . over the carpet.

Following blockers into the end zone

TIME-OUT

TONGUES OUT

SECOND HALF

BACK TO THE ACTION

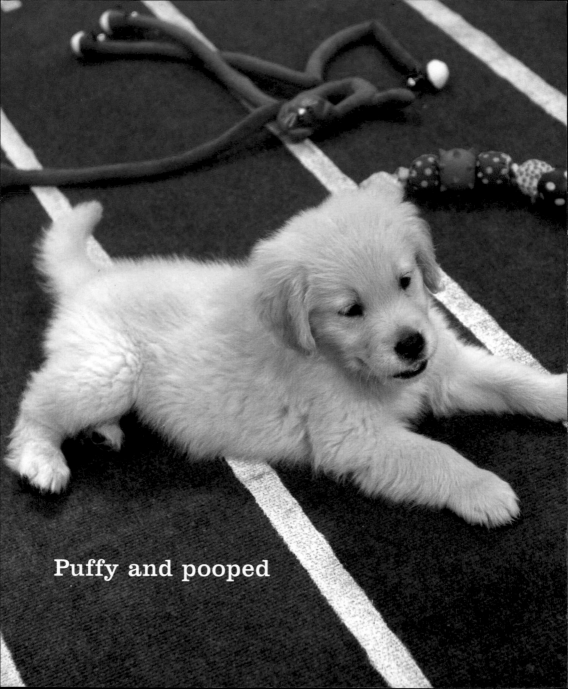

Puffy and pooped

Share, share is fair.

Too cute to tackle!

Could be my nap time.

The action is really picking up!

TIME-OUT

EARS UP

Number 39, out
of Brooklyn

Number 12,
who just flew
in from Fargo

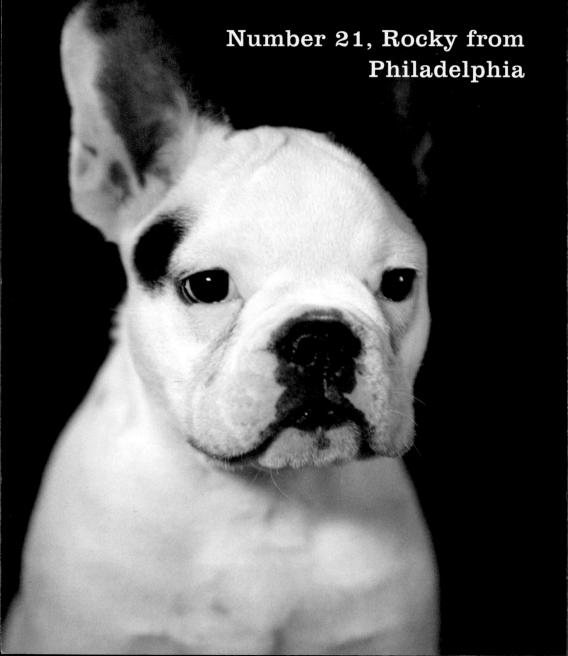

Number 21, Rocky from
Philadelphia

SECOND
HALF
THE FINAL STRETCH

The Puppy Bowl isn't all fun and games—though it is a ton of fun!

The dogs that take part are provided by dozens of adoption shelters and after each Puppy Bowl are available to be adopted into loving homes.

Thanks for being a fan of the Puppy Bowl and furry friends of all shapes and sizes!